ALSO BY ADRIAN CASTRO

Wise Fish
Cantos to Blood & Honey

HANDLING DESTINY

POEMS BY

ADRIAN CASTRO

COFFEE HOUSE PRESS
Minneapolis
2009

COPYRIGHT © 2009 Adrian Castro
COVER & BOOK DESIGN Linda S. Koutsky
AUTHOR PHOTOGRAPH © Pedro Portal

Coffee House Press books are available to the trade through our primary distributor, Consortium Book Sales & Distribution, www.cbsd.com or (800) 283-3572. For personal orders, catalogs, or other information, write to: info@coffeehousepress.org.

Coffee House Press is a nonprofit literary publishing house. Support from private foundations, corporate giving programs, government programs, and generous individuals helps make the publication of our books possible. We gratefully acknowledge their support in detail in the back of this book.

Good books are brewing at coffeehousepress.org

LIBRARY OF CONGRESS CATALOGING-IN-PUBLICATION DATA
Castro, Adrian, 1967–
Handling destiny : poetry / by Adrian Castro.
p. cm.
ISBN 978-1-56689-235-3 (alk. paper)
I. Title.
PS3553.A8153H36 2009
811'.54—DC22
2009020907

FIRST EDITION | FIRST PRINTING

1 3 5 7 9 8 6 4 2

Printed in the United States

ACKNOWLEDGMENTS

Some of these poems appeared in *Warpland: A Journal of Black Literature & Ideas, Black Renaissance Noire, Gulfstream, MiPoesias, Future Earth Magazine* (online journal), and *Asili* (online journal).

Handling Destiny was made possible in part by grants from NALAC Fund for the Arts, and Cintas Foundation.

For Ajíbọlá ọmọ mi, who has encircled my destiny.
For Ana Maria, who drew the circle.
For Ricardo and Caroline, who sit in the circle.

I. Yes, Dr. Williams

II. Handling Destiny

III. OTHER POEMS

I.

YES, DR. WILLIAMS

Apology

I'll go back
I'll go back one day
You have to understand this—
I didn't really leave my son

How can you love such a sergeant's daughter
Same man who planted pot
in my friend's pocket
sent him up for a two-year stretch
among swarms of dirty beans
liquid in their sting

And she was here
flower all bees come to kiss
I followed the summons
by water by train by train
to begin anew
Besides
the one who was conjured
from bones & water & salt
would have to be born here—

I'll say that
in my defense

TO BEGIN

. . . Home now
Furniture hugging walls
Chairs wooden in their embrace
Impressionists spine the bookshelves

There is a fat thoroughfare in the middle
I am open now
Anyone possibly knocking
I stand from window to window
cloth drawn
span the back doorway licking
the wind open
flora flipping conversations
The offering placed below
the bedroom window last night
now drunk with rain

This morning
I could see you
all over again

Under Construction

On this street opened—
hand fan disappearing nowhere—
layers of façade blown into rounded edges

Baroque buttresses—
Red tongue-in-groove stretch the door
iron hinge deadbolt hand knocking

Windows from sky to earth
slow yawn
of Caribbean morning

Café con leche rooster
strutting corn tassel feathers

No longer layers of each individual—
but now Home
erected into one

In this mixture a man ideals one perception
simple amid heaps & heaps of him

Café con leche: Sp. Coffee with milk mixture—cappuccino color.

Chewing Your Age

I'll go drop pounded medicine
                    now—
Elbowed on your door
brass is hinged still
with will to be new
white iron bars yawn—
                    (clearly a spike to open)
once & for last
or whatever iron sets its rust

Now mists your memory atop it
Now take
            your medicine—
Your unguent of burnt actions
And I'll be
alchemist of old age
hinged on your knees—

The Reality of
Tropical Depressions

Let's not wrestle with water
anymore—
Enters until we flexible
in its acceptance
Persistent in entering
through green or brown windowpanes
jagged from years of sun

Lights out
across the street yr candle
dances still or
flashlight we send
signals
interrupted by slinging branches
Tonight is o.k.—
after all
you walk by the window
tip yr head at the orange sky blue lightning
partially our rainbow

People not alone in the percussive squalls
(Caribbean music)
Sole leaf flicked by adolescent wind
gone

August 25, 2005

Direct Perception at the Forest

So much
depends
on the bank forming a river
and
river forming a bank

the red rooster courting
the marble hen
island sprouting in the middle
like new love

You must not cling to its bank fearfully
Moldy turtles slipping from
hollow roots—

formless in the end
free

The Threat of Rebirth
at Riverbank

"So that never in this | world will a man live well in his body | save
dying—and not knowing himself | dying;"
—*from* Paterson, *William Carlos Williams*

There is a month
        really
                just a moment or so
clay river cracked in ignorance
of its own dying—
Vulture circling to collect
        remnants
offerings
        to the Earth against dusty outcome
pushed by breeze
        really

Yet you sit at the shore
memory when eagle fished in one swoop
anticipating the next ship-
                ment
destined for your hands
        you'll shape it
                tongue to spell it down
only an opportunity
is what you ask—

from the corner of your eye
        head
                tilting at your friend
        mummied on the shore

In Cupped Hands

Give me your hands
since then
scarred
One day
something inside them—
Look
not around me
I'm not behind you
One day inside your
hands
you'll see something
inside:
I'll keep it in the brass bowl
below the candles near November Fourth

What Grows Among Refuse

Mushrooms shoot only to be snuffed
quickly
until jagged grass glistens around
like a city wall guarding itself
This morning
I wake dressed in dew
I will brush quietly the dried leaves
you have tossed on my gift
I will sleep insisting
like blooming jasmine
toll cacophonous victory
brass bell in hand
melody united
later—

By the River Acquiring Power

Let the chatter stop
already
The patches of rainbow meander
When you say
I say you—
I too was broken stained glass floating discarded
Now an overgrown root
every five years I must
return to trim
A river no matter how boulder
damns her path
over above it
flows no matter
the root stabbing the course

I will be flexible
I will take to form
like full glass of water

II.

Handling Destiny

HANDLING DESTINY:
THE SUPREMACY OF WATER

The thought like water
oracle to spill it—
There is blue on the roadside or
road reflecting blue
a stone too
planted like a Wednesday—
blue currents comb around it
in effect a swirl like destiny

They said once water is created
there will also be sand
an immovable stone to challenge it

Deep in the bush the cry is not
heard in the bush like birds
do not ruffle their wings
(ròbgò gàdà ròbgò gàdà)
Yet there is the
lone hunter with his hat's brim
hushing
If it wasn't for shadow
the mountain would not know how to walk

When the day came that sand
would grow gritty legs & sticky fingers
they told water to attach to nothing
motion saturates everything
They said it would reach home

In spite of having no
legs no

arms water
till this day
carries sand where it wants
mutable
should be the thought
oracle spills it so—

Ròngbò gàdà: Yòrubá. Onomatopoeic, describing, ruffle of wings.

Handling Destiny:
The Chieftaincy of Death

There is difficulty in handling a destiny
with so much dust—
      dust fills the tray
      dust in food drinks with dust
      dusty boots, guns, your eyes
      dusty
Night is dust
The day struggles to penetrate light
relentless, ambitious, organized
But here whimper of a dying soldier
the only moans from mothers both veiled & modern
the din of fear
merciless, chronic

And then there are times
only a dirge will trespass the dust
direct as is if riding on arrows to ears
of he whose breath encircles clouds
like in San Francisco
201 people sang directly at death
their breath a yellow arrow fashioned by tongues
(death is silenced by song)
A boy came crashing through the glass doors
shot
his shirt an abstract expression of city life
his brown bloodshot eyes opening wide
just making it to stay
a cloud pierced by song
another death postponed

Handling Destiny:
Two Knots Tied to Make a Rope

The handle of a hoe has a head but
lacks thinking
When each string is a shredded path
When each path lies across the river
calling you
showing its shiny teeth
you harvest these strings like knots
like white bulbs of cotton
like a farmer tying knots to form rope

When your calabash has shown cracks
seeps slow frustration
you bead a gourd with the net of costly years
of hollering at the ground
you shake it to make music
music when people meet & dance
you slap the bottom to echo pain
a chorus of hands clapping in counter time
like the climax of flamenco cante

You may ask
when the red earth has been trampled enough
when waves have hushed their inspirational lullaby
when the old man has circled the embroidered cloth
heavy with incantations
around his waist
penetrated the earth
as if saliva were sperm
when a certain palm tree with
red oily seeds sprouts
heavy with history

with incantations
an archive of our lives together
dancing singing praying
Yet the seeds are not what we're calling every morning
when the word pregnant with the crash of waves
silky sand kissing your beaten toes
awakens beauty like the dew on morning leaves

CODA

Faced with cultivating art
carrying baskets of water
at the mercy of gravity
subject to rot
like daggers hidden below earth
They created words of brass
stones symbolizing gods
words with the weight of history
refractive view into the heart
enticing the effects of your actions
(intrinsic subtle
brutally inexorable)
to come dance on your head
useful in its beauty

Handling Destiny:
Prayer on Four Tableaus

We begin with two
parallel lines from me to you
identical in movement
two trunks though really one who never meets
from me to you
you who can turn pebbles into salt
whose ears are wide enough for two to walk
You have carved your eyes atop now
hawk-like
you will witness this dialogue
in the end seal it like the scarification of birth
Eríwooò yà! Eríwooò yà! Eríwooò yà!

I leave the imprint on wood
a temporary scar
until breeze brushes it
a hand sweeps it
word enlivens it
silence transforms it—

Eríwooò yà: Yòrubá. Call to attention used by Babalawo
when beginning to chant divinational poems.

Invocation

When you see a gourd with water being carried
When you see a gourd being carried with water to its source
When you carry it toward light entering a window
When you see on your way to its source
the countless masks that have come before you
clothing tattered
horrible in their skin—
they've weathered what loss can do
what forgetting can do
what loneliness what ignorance
can do
They stood firm on a cultivated field
while sugarcane was sold before their eyes
while they scorched fields of families
before their very eyes

At first there were two
self-taught
identical in movement
who taught a few how to write
& taught a few how to read the scars on wood & skin
who in turn passed it on
who in turn passed it on to me—
to pray against those menaces circling
hawk-like
(cracked calabash
a thirsty river
shattered mirror
withered bones
clash of bones)
I tap the tablero tender
four tableaus (though really one)
identical in movement
delivering the message
from me to you
tender

Tablero: Sp. Wood tray, divination tray.

INCANTATION

Because word knows no posture
I write what I sing
Then I taste the dust
mounted on petition's face
I assure my tongue does not lie flat
word flies direct like three arrows
not knowing posture
I knock thrice at yr door
clear like an emergency
same door that opens baby's first tear
same door that drips seeds unto a field
door a knife opens on skin
door you opened when we met
late night
when all that light
came flooding

Now a strange vocation
to summon words soaked with rhythm
bathe you
collect yr sediment
recycle it like old roses into potpourri
words soaked with the dew of compassion

Dín dì ò mọ̀ nlọ girigiri
Dín dì ò mọ̀ nlọ girigiri
Dín dì ò mọ̀ nlọ girigiri
Wrapped in leaves placed on a dish we've made our petitions
as if to feed destiny itself
These two lines (though really one)
from me to you
now erased
they have never been permanent—
The child is leaving quickly
The child is leaving
quickly
The child is leaving
taking the petition to the other world

                                        *

A chameleon changes its skin when in danger
Don't carry water in a cracked calabash
Don't stare into shattered mirrors

Dín dì ò mọ̀ nlọ girigiri: Yòrubá. It's leaving fast.

Handling Destiny:
The Red Eyes of History

—for Kọlàwọlé Oshìtọlà

Itárúkú Itárúkú
Itàrùkù Itàrùkù
Rúkùrúkù tá tá tá
They wondered what
to do with time when it huddled into hamlet
pooled around forest of ficus
wearing ages of rings
A stream perusing the edge of bush
        it stops—
      becomes mirror
They gathered there notching
           the first market—Akésan

The road to Ọ̀yọ́
rickety in its cracked history
porcelain curse shot into empty space
winding through Ibàdàn Highway
like endless haze
Late smell of fried palm oil wicks
like dimming stars in a first-world sky
Roadside diviners selling verses in wisdom tongue
deep in the din of brass bells
brass throats cooled by sacrifice
red eyes encircled by chalk
the spray of gin moistening the mad dust

Four hours north of Lagos still
gaping hungry roads muddy
potholes like snares the size of slavery
large like revenge

springing corrupt cops
Ọ̀yọ́ springing bulbs of cotton along
a farmer's dream in Akéètan Báàlẹ̀
pooled around plantation of okra
The past still
tender & slippery

Big winged hands sprout from the center of Ọ̀yọ́
caressing shẹ̀kẹrẹ
like the world's oldest prayer
a gift of music to tufts of cloud
laced by native string beads & cowries
across the Aláàfin's palace of corrugated colonialism
encircling everyone by net of native string
united only when shaken a symbol
& masquerades chase shadows at high noon
But we stand poised balloon sized
half hands holding its base
       the world's oldest prayer
           tilting toward history
              an attempt
to grasp the run over traditions
before hoisted away by vultures
burnt blood carcass
before the old folks speak of tradition
like when waiting for the procession of a corpse

*

Dùndún drums invited for the coronation
of a Muslim Aláàfin—
they speak of past actions
when they squeeze the tension of their skin
when they beat their skin
          with curved sticks
At the coronation the Aláàfin
kneels before the Bàrà
where he meets the inevitable tattered cloth
masking the faces of past kings

cloth sewn to cover the mask of time
the guttural voice time

When he travels to Kósò
he is handed the weapons of Shangó:
  the double-headed axe carved from thundercelts
  snaps of stones at his fingertips flickering
  like frantic tongue of boa
  the secret of igniting song through speech
  dancing like brisk lightning bolt
          reaching for earth
  The rigid song of tyrants & the cult of personality
  Red velvet & curtains of raffia chalk
  charcoal camwood paints the walls
  encircling the Shangó shrine
—Does the king now wail Allah Akbar
does he still proclaim Kábíèsi o Ọbakósò?

From the outskirts of here
during the Ọ̀yọ́ Wars late nineteenth century
Yòrubá slaves
herded to Cuba & Brazil
& today
  we're writing on divination powder coded words
soaked with the dew of Caribbean soil
to be licked with red palm oil
Today jazz is dancing to shẹ̀kẹrẹ & bàtá rhythms
Today it is us who stare at the tattered mask
rags stiff as death
(strange inheritance we're carrying)
the load of the coffin maker's son
Where do we lay our colonial load?

The entrance to the Aláàfin's palace
still has medicines
ancient powders buried by the doors to return you
the favor of bad juju
verbs launched to burden your action

So we'll keep the music then
the collection of drums—dùndún, bàtá, igbin, bémbè,
gúdùgúdù—gathered
on the day they were all to compete
for the mouthpiece of the king
We'll take the music of orikì / verse
We'll take shèkèrè & shawórò too
shake their tongues at dancers
springing from the ground
dodging raindrops that fizzle to memory
Today's Òyó.
looking out the coffin maker's load
dodging raindrops on the procession of history

Itárúkú Itárúkú . . . : Yòrubá. Opening lines from the Odù Ifá Irosùn méjì
(Yòrubá divinational poem) narrating the origins of Òyó.

Akésan: Yòrubá. First market in Òyó founded with the town. Currently still
in operation.

Òyó: Yòrubá. Metropolis in Yorubaland linked to crucial moments in Yoruba
history. The king of Òyó was for a time considered the king of all Yorubaland.

Akéètan Báàlè: Yòrubá. Neighborhood near the palace of Òyó.

Shèkèrè: Yòrubá. Musical instrument whereby a gourd is strung with a net
filled with beads and cowrie shells.

Aláàfin: Yòrubá. The title of the king of Òyó.

Dùndún: Yòrubá. Hourglass, bimembraneous drums with strips of leather
from one drum head to other. These are squeezed to give different tones
while playing. Igbin, bémbè, gúdùgúdù are also types of drums.

Bàrà: Yòrubá. The mausoleum of past Aláàfin.

Shangó: Yòrubá. deity of thunder, fire. Also the name of the fourth Aláàfin,
so the current Aláàfin's ancestor.

Kábíèsi o Obakósò: Yòrubá. Hail his majesty the king of Kósò. Also the greet-
ing to the Aláàfin.

Bàtá: Yòrubá. Set of at least three hourglass bimembranous drums often
played for Shangó, or the Aláàfin.

Shawórò: Yòrubá. Small brass bells often strung to drums.

Ìbàdán: Yòrubá. Large metropolis in Yorubaland, Nigeria.

Handling Destiny:
How to Say Greetings

Greetings about yesterday
Greetings about today
of the two
greetings about both is best
The third day stands before you mirror-like

A horse painted like leopard with diviner
settled on top
mane waving at
                    passersby
Ram also with diviner on top
spiraled horns pointing at
                    passersby
                            in its own particular care
Today the careful serpent
        will not cross amid procession on the well-worn path

They ride toward the home
of a man troubled by cordiality
military bearded
known for forgetting
his father
his mother
They ride to advise him
he must greet them
& the ones who came before
even diviners
        who came before—
simple gesture of not forgetting
for sake of forward destiny
Serpent that treads

amid well-worn path
will have its backside snapped

Greetings about yesterday
Greetings about today
of the two
we will greet the dawn
the sunset everything
in between

Handling Destiny:
The Curse of the Coffin Maker's Son

1.
Let's paint our coffins white or
let's paint our coffins
red
while death sheds its suit of blood
shows us its shiny bones

When you go to the market
armed
the old people said
(a machete without footsteps)
to buy pumpkins to plant
nothing good can
come of it
Around here
we hide our fortunes inside pumpkins

2.
What to do when
the coffin maker's son
has set up shop
on your doorstep?
In the end
this is the central question
There is a bird cursed
to carry a coffin on his head
Take the toucan—
(I can stay with the parrot though
at worst he's condemned to repeat himself)
I have met people like this
atop highly decorated white horses

In fact they can never loosen their loads
even when the epigraph has ended

3.

Early one morning they called from the palace
Ọlọfin who wears a necklace of coral and jasper
like the world's intestines
gave us six pumpkins
             (a gift of no particular consequence)
Some dumped the pumpkins by the roadside
as their horses pranced
then some strapped them as children
planted them in the most barren garden

The Earth would sprout its guts out like a gift
Simple—
        Honest is a rich man
Grateful for simple
        is a rich man

Ọlọfin: Yòrubá. Title of the King of Ilẹ̀ Ifẹ̀. Lit. "Owner of the palace / law."

Handling Destiny:
Another Take on "The Emperor
Wears No Clothes"

Your home parched
sand dispersed desert
Your enemy your father's enemy too
a mirror for you to hop with hot feet

This morning the rumors clamored
raucous in their claims—
that you upon waking sit
& ponder your poop
that you bathe singing off-key
a salt 'n' pepper shower cap
you toss above your sparse head
People are talking—

In your dream a thirsty rooster cackles his gossip
tailfeather big as Texas
In your dream there were rivers cracked
trees winding down sparsely strangled vines
brown clouds of dusty death
turning morning to dusk

The old people who speak of death
called on the rainmakers—
      they said a rooster always crows early morning
      rain could not resist the call of frogs
      Shangó grants the wishes of orógbo
            (bitter kola)

Electric stones begin to rain
Double-headed hatchets as dance wands

The old people begin to dance—
We could see the liar licked by thunder
indelible mark on skin
a tattoo begging forgiveness

If not for words said backwards
your shower of fear
What will you say in your defense?
You squandered your home
You betrayed your brother
with an anvil & compass
You killed your children

Yet they never found
your weapons the fear you found
your secret revealed—
Daddy was sitting on the throne
all along
But you too
must one day lie
naked
a mere crest for a crown

Handling Destiny:
Tools of the Trade

I.

They make such uncomfortable clank
child of earth
child of fire
These are your tools of the trade
difficult when you use them

A large trunk with children darting
in all directions
appears slippery in its sheen
adorned with thorns

There comes a day in a man's life
when the machete he was given early on
can cut into small inheritances
place them in a large calabash
set them aflame
spill the ashes behind him
to cover his old footsteps
the one's he stepped over & over
trodden tongue lashing
the atlas of littered women
over & over every few years

2.

Remember at the end of seven days
a gift of hoe & machete
used at times by your grandfather
then again by his son
At the end of the seven days
remember the whipping song

as you with machete & hoe in hand
wrote on the earth diagrams
signatures that would sprout shelter
words won't lead you to obstacle's house

Remember
when she had a dimpled hammock on each thigh
marks from birth from years lying
behind
diagrams written on her history

Handling Destiny:
Declarations Against Birds
in the Night (ii)

If everyone were to be buried in coffins
the forest would be deplete of teak
If everyone struggled to dance with machete & bell in hand
cutting invisible birds in flight . . .
birds who at 2 a.m.
enter your pupils twitch
your dreams step mockingly on your terrain of hopes
There aren't many who have chosen
good lives—
sand does not reveal the footsteps of a madman
the rest of us are struggling

Wind often whips your tattered cloth
revealing shiny bones
the marks of time you keep
trying to conceal
The bloody cloth of disrespect for humans
charred amid shattered glass

They will arrive with their assorted plumage
dilating frequently
like iridescent memories
Sometimes a toucan
who carried coffin as beak
an owl subtle in her murmurous flight
Cat dainty night eyes
stealths her way to peruse
someone's pyramid of bones
There are times a woman
with small parcel of pounded powders

below knuckles knuckled worn knees
somewhere between
a spiderweb &
cracked mud wall hides it
She leaves with it
only to come back
with it naked
demanding
a do-over
like an ensemble playing in the key of buried love
She departs unwittingly after
eating her fill of gizzards
to gossip about with the music of waves of good-bye
empty in their songs
murmur hovering around slow salute of leaves waving to sleep
a cackle known only among these birds
noisy amid feathered eggs
& water gone sour
unfit to even wash your feet

Handling Destiny:
The Love Affair Between
Boat & Port

Over there vines twined rope-like
a boundary the way arms section love
Over here vines twined too
section off a dream safe
like waking with your wife

He launched from a beach
machete strapped hammer shovel
hoe in hand
that combed earth spiked
earth
stained it like a dead man
When you cast migration to sea
you must be armed against wind
water that bends your dreams
salt & sun that cures them slowly

On the day spirit
sullen on board sees port
the brass ring on the prow
fit like a wedding band
bursts its urge to dance
irresistible in its finger

Though water has washed footprints as witness
A promise was made at the beach some time ago—
we will see each other again
our arms now the distance between two
half circles

HANDLING DESTINY:
ON CROSSING BORDERS

We reinvent ourselves
sometimes counting beach pebbles
or landlocked cloth holding
water in place

The issue at hand—
Geography & who has access
Identity once you become ours
when crossing a pinup border
that marks you with whipping twigs
That is twigs—
   the first slave to ancestors
   the first to mast a mask of tattered breeze

At last in the Caribbean
we can begin—
   Indians dressed in aviary monarchy
   Spanish raiment chorizo'd by jade knife
      stolen at Olmec sculpture
   (Even African everything)
The cloth locked at your waist wading water
(Spanish was spoken here too)
illusory like thin blue pen on the ink of memory

Until tomorrow
another river peruses round stones stumbling
any río del Caribe
For instance a duck with waddling webbed feet
armor for feathers
(they say were the prototype for feet)
A border

of water & sand
all locked neatly in its cloth
an illusion of control
like sustained music of carnival

How do footprints know the future of their feet?
How does crooked beach know its balance of blue?
How does the moon get fooled by white curtain?
How does a child bereft
of history make his petition
acceptable to spirits?

With gravity as backdrop
more skin begins to reptile
Memories drip in collective mutiny
a parade of quetzal feathers drums stone calendars divination
instruments
Language cuts through the persistence of years
to form a clear
epitaph—
On another day we'll smile
with multicolored lips
showing our shiny leopard teeth

Handling Destiny:
The Initiation of the Butterfly

Grateful initiated butterfly
to be messenger of God—
not the one above (as they say)
but the one whose echo erupts into Earth

He stares at the omniscient elephant
whose tusks hang like lantern
like a funnel echoes summon—
that's where he asks his questions
There is a message hidden under
sacred seat / mat
Because he thinks he's alone
he in turn takes aim
his only revolver to solve
questions no one cares to answer
Revolver spinning
the way apple tumbles from head
Butterfly shoots roses (instead)—
burgundy bullets because
they seem the most beautiful
"I love
I do love," he says
"I'll begin again
after I've shed my little deaths—
I will love variously . . . "
"The need for religion" he says
"word   love   we"

At first they handed him
a mud ball
He stepped on it with left toe

Then swayed slowly
watching his step
till he buffed it ivory
sixteen seeds of ivory
with grooves like brain tissue

How to proceed
when the created seeds are your oracle?
The old man's poems are passed down
seven generations of words past
migrations wars
the noise of imported flags flapping

He will wake will wash his face his feet again
Cocoon himself with array of colored cloth
again
He will enter barefoot to step on reed mats
Walls white, green, blue, burgundy
yellow curtains fanning ripening fruit
Wrists & neck beaded like scars of honesty
He will sit with legs like slingshot
wooden tray between legs circular
tray carved around the edge
elephant tusks around the edge
carved
two turtles hobble hoarding homes
their heads meet at the head of carved tray

He will hold brass bell
stick on the right hand
again
He will open his sacred
wooden pot carved like the butterfly's flight
He will begin the chanting again
This morning good to greet
His masks his myths good to greet
He will wear honesty like a necklace of stone—

Butterfly
among the we of man
aware of where he is
in word with love with
we

HANDLING DESTINY:
APOLOGY FOR RETURNING

There still remains then—
Your head searches for the blessed bridge
that your feet won't yet take you

"I respect you & you respect me" said the dialogue
My approach was to unite
(I'll say that in my apology)

Reached the cold river wide
like groove around dead man's neck
like trench you leap while
delivering urgent message
(I apologize for my proximity to death)

My place being two blocks from Boulder Creek
Marine Street being so far from ocean
So I began my long walks around Arapahoe
"How to make poetry a divination?"
the way an exile must invent his home

Two blocks away I could hear
the slow trickle of seasons—
Not like Miami
where green, blue, orange
are scattered by heat
the all embracing heat year long
Snow has a way of muffling motion
The echo of heartbeat hides
Not like Miami
where pulse turns words into projectiles
with accents

Then someone said I would not eat
I thought maybe the novelty of outsider
my skin too distracting
But in the mouth of a poisoned arrow
there's always the hunter's breath
though I didn't know quite how to shoot
though I had a quiver of bilingual leather

I brought palm oil & the memory of fried plátanos
my mother's moros
It was then my feet began to stir
from the deep rhythm of home
I could hear words from childhood
in a chorus of memory
soundtrack not yet harmonic
I cannot apologize for taking what is mine
the way a mockingbird steals
language

Because rhythm has no ego
(who owns music of breath?)
I listened to the crack of drums in my sleep
my head to carry my load
to a white stone where there were
chiseled sixteen markings
a footprint that fit my foot
In the dream I would wash this stone with herbs
like Sabe Lección, Siempre Viva, Maravilla
Now I'd have to memorize these marks
make words then articulate them—

Anyone can jump a dry river at night
but who would be owl's messenger
It was then I vowed to be attendant
at the bridge
at best to make music
out of colors crossing the other side

In Yòrubá, émèrè is a child that dies
is reborn & again . . .
I apologize for my necessary deaths
There still remains then—

But I am home

Plátanos: Sp. Plantain

Moros: Sp. Rice & black beans cooked together. A Caribbean specialty.

Sabe Lección: Sp. Different herbs. Literally, "learn lesson," Always alive,"
"Marvelous."

Émèrè: Yòrubá. Child that's born then soon dies, then is reborn.

Handling Destiny:
Snapshot: Ibàdàn, Nigeria, 4 a.m.

In America the call to prayer is private
muffled in mosaic halls of mosques
mega-churches that sprout like suburbs

They wake you early in Ibàdàn—
the call to prayer public as poverty
not like the autochthons
whose homes are sacred spaces
the echo of secrets buried
the stomp of children
laughter opening windows to the sky

They've arrived again at Ibàdàn
calling for conversion with bullhorns
Religion born from
the ground up cut
the imagination
cut
the way running you fall into hidden pit

They should explain their purpose
their finger-pointing judgments
their threatening cloth
and the corruption cascading off dirt roads

Handling Destiny:
Òfún Twice Again (Revisited)

*"The work will be in the realm of the imagination as plain as the
sky is to a fisherman—"*
from Spring and All, *William Carlos Williams*

"Ọmọde ó tikú"—
murmured el negro viejo after his spirit mounted someone's
head (Ègúngún). The spirit from another era, tiempo de la colo-
nia, tiempo de seseribó, de los negros Kongo, negros Lúkumí
(Ègúngún). He said he knew the story—

Perhaps these were the last words he ever heard before the new
pact was made. They said it would be of utmost importance for
him to observe the taboo of not blowing out candles. The candle
would be the measure, the vehicle of communication between
Ikú & himself—blowing out the flicker would sever the dialogue.
There would come a day when he would see a candle burning at
someone's bedside. As an herbalist & diviner he could not heal
that person. Ikú would need that life; probably so that another
one could be born somewhere else.

There was actually a time, maybe this is still going on, when a per-
son's Orí inù (that is, literally the "head inside," the entity within
that says "do this" or "do that," that says "follow this way," "no,
turn here"), would choose where & when it was going to be born,
to whom, who would be the patron deity / òrìshà, what course his
life would follow, and finally when will he breathe his last sigh. This
of course would be contingent on what kind of destiny, what kind
of head the Orí inù chose—Orí ire or Orí bùrùkú, good or bad
head. But then sometimes a head chooses to be born & to die soon
after & born & die & continue this cycle—the head of an abíku.

There was actually a time, maybe this is still going on, when before burying the abíku, someone (the parents, priests presiding over this ritual) would clip a piece of ear from el niño's corpse or cut half a pinky. The idea was to identify him as abíku when he returned (and they always return). If he has such markings his history, the paths he traversed, the heads he's petitioned, would be known. The proper amuletos can be prepared, the taboos observed. Somewhere along the lines though, the Orí inù in conjunction with his patron deity & Ègúngún / ancestors must all make a pact with Ikú.

Durówojú actually wants to live.

The Pact / Imulè:
1.
The candle will be our medium for dialogue
We must always
be on speaking terms

2.
When you see the candle by the bedside burning
it will be my message to you:
Do Not Touch!

3.
You will heal through herbs &
the words I give you to
spray into the solution

4.
Never dress in black
I may mistake you for
someone ready to die

5.
As much as possible
do not speak wickedly or curse anyone
I will remedy any transgressions

6.
As much as possible stay away from funerals
I like to work alone
Death is death's work (Ikú ni ikú she)

7.
Ègúngún will be my messenger
along with the departed wise
who knew the secret of walking with cane

8.
You may also petition me
through that white staff
the one with bells & snail shells

9.
Do not be tempted by beads & titles
The valuable ones
you'll obtain by your performance

10.
Remember this pact
& I will give you yr name
& vision form the hilltop

All this was negotiated just prior to Durówojú's birth. He probably kneeled before the Owner of the Sky while Ikú, the inumerable Ègúngún, and his patron òrìshà sat watching with fly-whisks in hand and full regalia (after all, one of their own was about to embark on his journey).

He probably placed in circular fashion inside a big calabash all his choices, probably whispered into the gourd a slow "tó a ba là Eshù." We say probably because one thing is for sure, he does not remember the details. In fact no one remembers the details of their creation. No one remembers their destiny, the mission they chose, their personal òrìshà, and most importantly the date of their last breath.

Memory & continuity. Keeping el hilo de la conversación. Never losing the wavy & fragile link that keeps you grounded to yr root. The dialogue with the spirits that may tap yr left shoulder & all that. But no one remembers. No one remembers! Esto no es fácil!!!

In order to recall the details of what went on in the other world, to map his destiny, Durówojú must be taken for divination. And even then one session won't do it. The story will get revealed as his life turns the page & changes rhythm & the oracle is cast several more times. So they took him to the babalawo Awopìtàn's house. After pouring libations & reciting the necessary prayers & incantations—greeting the creator, those who came before him, the divination, earth, wind, river, ocean, jungle, & crossroad deities—Awopìtàn cast the divining chain / òpèlè used by babalawo. A picture began to emerge of the paths he's crossed. He said Òrúnmìlà, the divination deity, has given us certain verses & stories to deliver messages regarding the rhythms of our lives. He said Durówojú patron deity was Òrúnmìlà but he will always have an affinity with Ògún, the deity of creativity, iron, and war, and also Òshun, the divinity of rivers, fertility, and arts. But most prominent is his close relationship with ancestors Ègúngún, Ikú's messengers. He said it would be through a kinship with the past that he would accomplish his most difficult tasks; even the art of divination and verse chanting. He will be a mouthpiece for those who came before.

Awopìtàn said he had a predisposition to a vivid imagination. Because of this there will be mysterious phenomena happening to him like visions & dreams of secret songs. He will not regard them as strange.

He said Durówojú should be taught even at an early age the rigors of an herbalist. He should be taught at least how to recognize certain trees & plants, their healing properties, their harvesting times, how they mix & with what substances. All this will eventually lead to an encyclopedic knowledge not only of their medicinal qualities but of their ability to alter the invisible rhythms that underlie most things.

Awopìtàn said there will be certain medicines that must be prepared so as to begin bridging the gap between this world and that world. The goal was communion with the deities on a regular basis. Awopìtàn would need to establish el niño's head well in this world so he would not leave again till the day he chose. He chanted in Yòrubá something like,

> "we never hear of the death of a hoe,
> of the death of cloth,
> of the death of earth,
> until they are very old"

His head secured by word & medicine, morsels of ashé, the invisible sunshine behind life, planted to sprout into a well-lived life. Awopìtàn fastened a brass chain around his left ankle too. (There is always the detail of Ikú being overprotective. The relationship is like playing with a leopard—even an affectionate jab from its paw will leave a scar). All this to give him a strong foundation, to then sustain the load his destiny will make him hoard.

We were witness to this event. We heard what needed to be done. There was actually a time, maybe this is still going on, when people consulted with the spirit world, the other world, home some call it, on such occasions as the third day after birth. We named him Durówojú, "stay with us so we see the blessings of life." We collected the ingredients that would shape his destiny & began to assemble them.

The citizens of the other world are aware of the images & subtle rhythms that stories & verse evoke that run through our lives. Awopìtàn said that barring some details of modernity, his life would follow a certain ancient story pertaining to the divination—

Òfún is like this /
Òfún ni jẹ bẹ—

The page continues to turn. The rhythm, the rhythm will come from dreams.

Ọmọde ó tikú: Yòrubá. The child has died.

Abíku: Yòrubá. Another name for Émèrè.

El hilo de la conversación: Sp. Literally, keeping the thread of the conversation.

Durówojú: Yòrubá. Proper name meaning "Stay with us to see."

To a ba la Eshù: Yòrubá. Any indelible mark on Esu. Often said to "seal" rituals and prayers.

Awopìtàn: Yòrubá. Name meaning the "Babálawo narrates history."

Babalawo: Yòrubá. Priest of Ifá specializing in divination, poetry, medicine. Considered senior priests due to their training and knowledge.

Ashé: Yòrubá. Multidimensional word meaning power, "Amen," said at the end of prayers and blessings. the invisible pulse of animate and inanimate objects.

Seseribó: Efik. Refers to specific regalia among the Abakná/Efik descendants in Cuba. This entire sentence comes from a Rumba song.

III.

OTHER POEMS

PETITION AT ÒSHUN RIVER, OSHOGBO, NIGERIA

—for my mother

The swirling cement sculptures yellow with years
propped along meandering path
sneaking toward the orange river
A path is what we call the earth that lies trampled
And this forest pregnant with ẹdun—red colobus monkeys
who wear brass ẹdan
as necklace to guarantee survival—
Here at home
He who has brass has blessings
The echo of agógó gongs reverberate
the echo of brass fans shaped like fish kissing the thick air
This is the spot my mother was born
kneeling
     naked
          praying like a mother for her child's life

Once they arrived fleeing aggressors with indigo turbans &
horseback
The collection of stones pricked their knees
Fingers clenching thumb
the left hand above right
as they petitioned the river for peace
A fish with five red parrot feathers for fins
chorused the petition
squirted a response on a few of their faces

Now at the gateway open twin brass doors
fish & people-like figures swell from metal
they welcome women who come carrying calabashes
in the name of fertility & community

in the name of power
in the tradition of creating form from water
At the gateway stand several masquerades
cemented with panels of cowry shells
which when kissed by the sun
seem like mirrors saying
you are history happening—

(Having come from across the waters
survived the onslaught of man
to re-tell history with your words—)

You arrive at the riverbank with certain leaves selected
throughout Oshogbo
an empty calabash black
soap
You wash your head kneeling
to form it like water
shapeless & necessary
The feathered fish streams its response
rinses the black soap
you petition again for peace

This the place my mother gave birth
kneeling
            naked
                  praying
            like a mother for her child's life

                                        —Oshogbo-Miami

_____

Ẹdun: Yòrubá. Red colobus monkeys.

Ẹdan: Yòrubá. Brass male and female figures about six inches long linked at
the head by a chain. They are the symbol of community for the traditional
Yòrubán Ogboni society.

Agógó: Yòrubá. Type of gong or bell often played with stick.

Place Where Whirlwind Lives

Where they end their spin—
strip of soggy grass invaded by water
intercoastals sequestered by
large glass sculptures transparent in case of impermanence
sprouting like fire hydrants
on Ọyá's cinnamon spine
This season there have been
four attacks
bearing male & female names

When life begins here
ebb of memory from here
an immigration of pulse lashing at the lush green orange
honey dripping dreams
(You should be lucid in your dreams)
That's why you've come here—
Camilo
Mr. Cartwright
Jean Baptiste
Or perhaps it was
vine of bitter momordica /
cundiamor we call it
bitter for blood entwining past injuries
After all
more likely spirits encircled back home
danced & dressed
will come here too
flora being the same Caribbean
same West African

She then gathered fallen leaves, fallen skin of
chameleon
changed them to burnt words—

perhaps vengeance for her children's capture
Whirlwinds keep coming
springing like incantations
projectile from witch-woman's hand
(our mother) that even
a king was borne by a woman

From West Africa they depart
soft soothing breezes looking for home
gather strength
pulse whirl dripping
dreams into water
sucking you & me

Ọyá: Yòrubá goddess of wind, tornados, wife of Shangó,
the god of thunder, fire.

Cundiamor: Spanish. Bitter herb. *Momordica balsamica* botanical name.

Declarations Against Birds in the Night (1)

If you ever heard an owl wail
at night you
know nothing good can come of it
They say back home
someone will soon fall
a tree a powdered death
There will be news cracked
jagged like clay river
Then there are violent acts such as
sleeplessness
which fracture your course slowly
Back home if at 2 a.m.
birds are still singing
a hearing is at stake—
decisions are being made regarding
someone's cycle whether
that song will inspire an image
whether eggs sheltered under sand
will hatch a new horizon—

at the meeting between blood & bone
the meeting between fruit & tongue

When Hearing Bàtá Drums . . .

Atandá they say
had the secret
(wrapped in red cloth)
to speak in goatskin
beat a message spiraling into sound
straight to the ears which woke destiny
red rooster's first flutter of wings
first cackle
not wake yet
—the rise of early freedom
    when he woke at four a.m.
        kneeled once on knee
    leather strip in hand
        reciting history
            praise names to remind that we came
                from somewhere

        When we entered our hollowed tunnel
Atandá was standing at the end
hands callused
when we heard the guttural sounds
    the ki-gún call
(there was also Ño José, Obakole, Akinlakpa)
when we waking the Caribbean sun

These bàtá carved like hourglass
speak because of tension on skin
squeezing the bandages of injured history
Once you fell a trunk
you must give it voice—
bitter as cedar or
sweet like almendra
wrap it in red cloth

bury it deep within the trunk
voice will echo from tunnel
out the bass end the
other crisp slapping end keeping time

myriad of words
    impregnating rhythm in them
    the flavor of who we are
    our history rhythmic
    bitter & sweet
    hard but
    ours

Atandá: Yòrubá. Proper name of one of the first drummers brought to Cuba
as a slave. Famous for consecrating the first set of bàtá drums in Cuba. Ño
José, Obakole, Akinlakpa were other historical drummers.

Almendra: Sp. Almond.

Song of Chameleon

I have sinned in front of mirrors
But I'll say this
in my defense—
Too scared to face my indecency
the voice with a larynx
big as mangoes too—
I took your voice burnt with tabaco
They say you must first imitate
before your tongue
jagged in novice
can ripen a word
shape it along color
before words being enough
change what's before you

Now
squeezing the bandages of injured history
when they hid your clothing
from the riverbank
slings of leather like slices
stretched along your skin
in the mood of talking drum
you remember only when they
tighten
speak from tension after all

It's time for your dissertation
mirrored cool one more color
on the chameleon's back
Time to play forgive the rainbow
your song of imperfection

ITUTU SANKÓFA 2003

for the memory of Ramon "Mongo" Santamaria

There will be people
        they said back in January
        that will leave us depart
while looking back at their people
—they said travelers from afar
we will see each other again—

One crisped a melodic conga solo
even while casket being lowered
after eighty-three years of
flying forward Sankófa-like
(bird who flies while looking at history)

Beginning when "Afro-Blue"
inspired from a chant praising Ọbatálá
deep in the din of echoes
in Jesus María, La Habana
sounds that permeated cloth walls of el barrio's history
of central de azúcar, café, tabaco
like the scent of sopa de quimbombó
bollitos de caritas
proclaiming their scent through baroque streets
You flying forward while looking at history

In the time of "Watermelon Man"
you leaped through lines yr new country
was not willing to cross
You with golden rope of Santa Bárbara hanging
from yr neck entwined
in glass beads & sweat
thunder rolling from caramelo hands
celebrating how man is man—
"la clave no tiene color mi hermano"

said yr drum-stained hands, Mongo
when they lowered la caja
yr last dance to a young rumbero's llanto
the goatskin's lament praising
how you looked back into history
flying forward

A faint solo begins to play now
deep in el otro mundo
only you
can now chorus a response
kind of music you hear on tufts of clouds
yr quiet chorus now echoes here
where many mimic yr rhythm

Lying by your casket
was a red feather from an African Grey parrot
        (symbol of messengers)
though we're not in Cuba anymore
we're not in Africa anymore
still a red feather to chorus yr response

You keep flying forward
Sankófa-like
looking back into history at us
        your people

Itutu: In Afro-Cuban/Yòrubá religion, burial rites for initiates; a sacrifice to
cool, and /or right a wrong.

Ọbatálá: Yòrubá. Diety of white cloth, purity, peace.

Azúcar: Sp. Sugar.

Quimbombó: Sp. Okra.

Bollitos de caritas: Sp. Fritters made from black-eyed peas.

La caja: Sp. The box, casket.

llanto: Sp. Lament.

Rumbero: Sp. Rumba musician.

INCANTATION FOR DANCER

I raise my arms snake-like
In one hand hangs brass bell
the other beaded fly-whisk
My head is smooth today
I can display red coral beads
      coiling into heaps
Today I will nourish my navel with morsels of destiny—
      today fish
           river water that molds its own course
      tomorrow wash it with leaves of baobab
Today my feet will not step
on a wicked man's heels
I can feel red sand from home inching
between my toes
Forward to the white crest above inching its edge out
to partner with illumined stars

The Fickle Nature of Friendship

We are not interested
in erecting glass homes
jagged angles to slice your hand

The neighbors
are sloppy with their stone garden
& prayers are unreliable
until their bones crash with bones—

Then we can begin
an earnest conversation of our time:
I will show you my hand with five bones
You show me yours

Then there is water
crisp like brass from a blacksmith's well—
it takes the form of our cupped hands

planted
in a garden only what glistens can see

THE BLUES OF HANDLING DESTINY

—after Yusef Komunyakaa

When you juggle roses
in cupped hands
in spite of yr gold rings
you believe it's only the beginning
This the first time
you step out onto the crossroads—

Yet there have been
times you've
been out of breath
only to come back to yourself
yourself mirrored
steps always go
back
to yourself—

There are times you caress
a head with a nail for a crown
feathers
and needles are sewn into that
crown
when you step out onto the crossroads

There are times they are chosen for you
There are times you kneel and choose
your calabash of destiny
change it only when born again
when you step out onto the crossroads

Song to Remember a Loved One

We are looking for you
We are looking for you
We've searched on the trampled path
We've searched below the ochre earth

We're returning with a light load on our backs

We are looking for you
We are looking for you
We've asked the citizens who inhabit solitude
We've asked citizens who carve smiles on the door of night

We're returning with a light load on our backs

We are looking for you
We are looking for you
We've cooked morsels with stories laced in their scents
We've cooked gourds of ajiaco & mixed memories

We're returning with a load wrapped in song
We're returning with a voice deep like the murmur of years
loved

Ajiaco: Sp. Hearty soup of various meats, viands, and other ingredients.

THE CACTUS KISS

1.

I am the cactus kiss kid
I have a pocket full of needles
I am the older brother of knife

I called you again to pluck the apple
from the cactus you asked,
"How do we reach such redness?"

You with lips that splash
& break at the your feet like
the morning we woke on the beach

I am the cactus kiss kid I tell you
praying for rain at the shrine of the hot Earth
A fireman with a long long beard

2.

I don't know if I can tell
any difference between
my father & me

> I tell my daughter:
> do not alight there, wait
> not there either
>
> I tell my daughter:
> the bird that glistens in your eyes
> never steps on spurs

3.

My face hardened by heat & humidity
handled by irony
the way snake shapes river of clay

I handle a clay face with shells
for eyes two fish eagle feathers
atop you can say permanent kind of crown

the wind as beak
& necklace of needles

For/Against: A Dialogue

Before today
understand for against
I knew you years
so often kicking the earth open
You sit stooped on steps
legs not what they were
right angled facing hollow ground—
Beginning how your father never really
loved someone
hurled your olive skin across the room for instance
so once you said it you said it
always
With you a duel was quick
iron flicks of the forked tongue
your hammered hands
you didn't need to touch her
your leopard eyes smelting
red machetes enough
Now I'm facing you smiling:
You Are Me

I've given you basic hand signals, he said—
go duel
upon the sand
Here's the knife
running down your DNA
red with forged eyes
(but today caressing the earth open)

INCANTATION FOR THREE

—for Ana Maria

The curse has ended
I declare my life to fly but
with wings tranquil
hovering
over remnants of sacrifice

When I was coming
back—
I
voiced the spectacle simple
nothing new
declared it residue
called it
place where you deposit such things

We gather sorting through
dead memories
picking the choicest
for best digestion
I have yet to see a young vulture

Complete—
you complete—having
yet seen a young-looking vulture:
bald head wobble walk
perusing through
old sacrifices

Good-bye for now—
memory of there
mists through feathered mind

It will be cool with you
lasting like cast brass
For you
me
& the kids—

A.N.A.'s Revenge

Talcumed by betrayal
yet again
a slash on the comfort
of skin
Yet we draw the drapes today
a smile opening
the sun under the watch of your caress
Yes it is possible
after the onslaught
an immense negative
spiraling to nowhere
a pool deserted by bitterness
mango opened unripened
stringy core clinging acidy
dangling with hope
It is possible
to smile once again
peruse our leather canvases
like the curl of rainbow cresting into climax
kind & loving
a spirit riding two lines
vertical from heaven to you
and me to you

What Name Is In / Ìkọsẹ̀dáyé

Red earth grounded in blood
          long sacrifice
Along with constant oil palm trees
arms outstretched dripping
          generous red oil
dripping sonorous words into soil
paving a path to the source—
this where word, witness, & creation meet
          (what name is in)—

There are histories spinning on carousel
revealing origins in circular dance—
          "Born while kneeling"
          "Child who has beauty"
          "Death will not take this one"
          "We have seen you before"
          "The child has come home"
incantation in name
amulet for future
guardian
like cervical erected in your person
shadow like a name
          (what name
                    is in)—
When you've forgotten where
& among you came
more a problem of illness
more like
          muffled music
like incomplete thought between
flesh & blood not
          orphan
not quite fetus

a bastard bone
    what name is in—

For us likely to come from ikin seeds
ikin can speak of origins
sights unseen on the way to creation
marks of birth
at the kneeling of creation
choosing the calabash containing ingredients to shape your destiny
Marks on the face map-like
etched at birth
For us
likely to describe spirit residing in head
this is
what name is in—
a text to call your own
complete clear
like the tonal drum
stretched & beaten
at your naming ceremony
Ìkosèdáyé
. . . echo in the vastness of history

Ìkosèdáyé: Yòrubá. Naming ceremony, baptism, and divination done within
the first week of birth.

Ikin: Yòrubá. Palm nuts from the Oil Palm tree believed to be the representa-
tion, after properly consecrated, of Òrúnmìlà, òrìshà of knowledge, wisdom,
divination, and witness to creation.

Prayer for Naming Ceremony

—for my daughter Ajíbọlá

Today we wake to touch forehead on Earth
Today we wake with brow burrowed into the richness of hope
Today early when dew feet
spread through the theater of daylight
we pray that
at the night of our lives you will
witness our last ritual

She is three days old today
& steps thrice on the dust of the world
Can we differ the foot of madman
from the print of prince?

(We have assembled herb bundles—
        Ọdúndún here called siempre viva
        Tẹ̀tẹ̀ called bledo / wild spinach which
        sprouts despite the pounce of man
        Atẹ̀pẹ̀ / Gbegi the grass that twines
        through contorting obstacles
We have bundled on clay dish what you will taste:
kola nuts, bitter kola, sugarcane, honey, pepper,
dried fish, water, gin, red African-Grey feather as spoon)

Today we begin to sketch the verses
you will sing through life
Verses that you chose in the language of deities
when you kneeled in the other world
when I exhaled liquid fatherhood
& your mother embraced my breath
We pray that we may plant a flag
so you know where is home

even after the pounce of madmen
We pray that you are careful where to alight
that you fly forward while
looking back
That your verses do not scatter if
a storm tears your memory
That you understand the songs you will sing
And you remember the language you once spoke

Today is the opening chapter
of a crystallized prayer

After "Naima"

Since opening you I've learned the first word
mercy
first sheet of sound to shelter
from broken light
the way sheets come between man & woman
I keep trying to understand your harmony
how your speech breaks
in the middle of your thought
(I gotta tell you when
you take off your half moon earrings
the night table hung
between a crush & marriage
I remember how your Caribbean atlas
displays your humid history

ONTOLOGICAL AFRO LOGIC

"There are too many
spirits lying in the ocean"
says Olúwò

Water in spite of having
no legs no
arms

has made sand of them bones

Olúwò: Yòrubá. Head of Babalawo traditionally selected based on experience,
knowledge, and reputation. Also the head in the Ogbọni Fraternity.

OLD PEOPLE'S CREDO

A bearded narrator
a pair of dropped breasts
in Ijẹbú
reclining on the cool of wisdom
rolled leaves of tába
pressed on purple lips—

The slender tree above the canopy
dress multi-colored
The rainbow sighs like
sky's necklace
Earth watches with gaping eyes
the menace of dirt
among the many murmurs
The stain of man
on brass sunlight fogging
the opaque glass to the other story too
The menace of murmur
soils your brass mind too
glass divides this world
& that world—

They said
wrap yourself in cloth cloud
to detect the slightest
breeze
& the dust that tags along
yr eyes to remain like glass
as you walk to the shore

Ijẹbú: Yòrubá. Place and Yòrubá ethnic group.

Tába: Yòrubá. Tobacco.

The Origins of the Owners of Land

—for the members of Oshugó Àgàn

At first a child
rolled off a reed mat
a height of no consequence
Later the bald ageless vulture
circles the hill the man climbs

When the owners of the land arrived
they brought beaded bag in their search
Bag beaded big enough to house the echoes
that gave birth to sketches of words on dust
Bag deep enough to circle obstacles
that would sprout upon birth

They reached a clean house chalked walls
of peace a person of peace
They planted a pair of brass scepters
illumined male / female
short legs kneeling long torso crisscrossed
by arms
hands
clenching some secret
or just its thumbs

They saw three to be balanced—
  Earth & us
  Impermanence & love
  water & its gourd as gorge
  fish & whirling water

How they all seemed dependent on each other
There is balance where there are three . . .

COLOPHON

Handling Destiny was designed at Coffee House Press, in the historic
Grain Belt Brewery's Bottling House near downtown Minneapolis.
The text is set in Spectrum.

FUNDER ACKNOWLEDGMENTS

Coffee House Press is an independent nonprofit literary publisher. Our books
are made possible through the generous support of grants and gifts from
many foundations, corporate giving programs, state and federal support, and
through donations from individuals who believe in the transformational
power of literature. Coffee House receives major general operating support
from the McKnight Foundation, the Bush Foundation, from Target, and from
the Minnesota State Arts Board, through an appropriation by the Minnesota
State Legislature and from the National Endowment for the Arts. Coffee
House also receives support from: three anonymous donors; the Elmer L. and
Eleanor J. Andersen Foundation; Bill Berkson; the James L. and Nancy J.
Bildner Foundation; the Patrick and Aimee Butler Family Foundation; the
Buuck Family Foundation; the law firm of Fredrikson & Byron, PA.; Jennifer
Haugh; Anselm Hollo and Jane Dalrymple-Hollo; Jeffrey Hom; Stephen and
Isabel Keating; Robert and Margaret Kinney; the Kenneth Koch Literary
Estate; Allan & Cinda Kornblum; Seymour Kornblum and Gerry Lauter; the
Lenfestey Family Foundation; Ethan J. Litman; Mary McDermid; Rebecca
Rand; the law firm of Schwegman, Lundberg, Woessner, PA.; Charles Steffey
and Suzannah Martin; John Sjoberg; Jeffrey Sugerman; Stu Wilson and Mel
Barker; the Archie D. & Bertha H. Walker Foundation; the Woessner Freeman
Family Foundation; the Wood-Rill Foundation; and many other generous
individual donors.

 This activity is made possible
in part by a grant from the
Minnesota State Arts Board,
through an appropriation by the
Minnesota State Legislature
and a grant from the National
Endowment for the Arts.

NATIONAL
ENDOWMENT
FOR THE ARTS

MINNESOTA
STATE ARTS BOARD

TARGET.

To you and our many readers across the country,
we send our thanks for your continuing support.

Good books are brewing at www.coffeehousepress.org